LIGHTHOUSES

CAROL M. HIGHSMITH AND TED LANDPHAIR

CRESCENT BOOKS

NEW YORK

Photographs copyright © 2000
by Carol M. Highsmith
Text copyright © 2000
by Random House Value Publishing, Inc.
All rights reserved under International and
Pan-American Copyright Conventions.

No part of this book may be reproduced or
transmitted in any form or by any means
electronic or mechanical including photo-
copying, recording, or by any information
storage and retrieval system, without
permission in writing from the publisher.

This 2000 edition is published by
Crescent Books, an imprint of
Random House Value Publishing,
a division of Random House, Inc., New York.

Crescent is a registered trademark and
the colophon is a trademark of
Random House, Inc.

Random House
New York•Toronto•London•Sydney•Auckland
www.randomhouse.com

Printed and bound in China

Library of Congress Cataloging-in-Publication Data
Highsmith, Carol M., 1946–
Lighthouses /
Carol M. Highsmith and Ted Landphair.
p. cm.
ISBN 0-517-20877-6
1. Lighthouses—United States Pictorial works.
I. Landphair, Ted, 1942– . II. Title.
VK1023.H34 2000   99-37451
387.1'55'0222—dc21   CIP

8 7 6 5 4

Project Editor: Donna Lee Lurker
Designed by Robert L.Wiser, Archetype Press, Inc.,
Washington, D.C.

*The authors express particular appreciation to
Cullen Chambers, director of the Tybee Island,
Georgia, Historical Society and a nationally
prominent lighthouse restoration authority, for
graciously sharing his expertise on lighthouses
and lighthouse lore.*

*We also wish to thank the following
for their generous assistance in connection
with the completion of this book:*

Assunta's Restaurant
Slidell, Louisiana

Brennan's Restaurant
New Orleans, Louisiana

Comfort Inn
Sault Ste. Marie, Michigan

Creekwood Inn
Michigan City, Indiana

Crowne Plaza
Rochester, New York

Eliza Thompson House
Savannah, Georgia

Foley House Inn
Savannah, Georgia

Galatoire's Restaurant
New Orleans, Louisiana

Hampton Inn
Duluth, Minnesota

Main Street Inn
Hilton Head, South Carolina

Omni Royal Crescent Hotel
New Orleans, Louisiana

R. Keith Bradley
International Paper Realty Corporation,
Haig Point, South Carolina

Christie Caloudas
Hilton Head Island, South Carolina,
Chamber of Commerce

Nicole and David Dickson
Folsom, Louisiana

Daniel J. Donarski Jr.
Sault Ste. Marie, Michigan,
Convention and Visitors Bureau

Patty Donoghue
Greater Rochester, New York,
Visitors Association

Joseph Jakubic
International Chimney Corporation,
Buffalo, New York

Stacey Kellogg
La Porte County, Indiana,
Convention & Visitors Bureau

Marc and Rosemarie Kuhn
Plantation, Florida

Carlton McKinney
Edina, Minnesota

Pat Shinn
Duluth, Minnesota,
Convention & Visitors Bureau

Jenny Stacy
Savannah Area Convention & Visitors Bureau

Nina Stack
Block Island, Rhode Island, Tourism Council

Boatswain's Mate 1st Class Scott Stanton and Machinist's
Tech 3rd Class Jeremy Rohanna
U.S. Coast Guard, Boston Light

Pat Tuttle
Hospitality Tours of Savannah, Georgia

Bonnie Warren Public Relations
New Orleans, Louisiana

Wayne Wheeler
President, United States Lighthouse Society

FOREWORD

It has been said that lighthouses, probing the eternal, mysterious sea, are to America what castles are to Europe. Satellite and radio navigational aids have rendered lighthouses obsolete to big shippers and sophisticated recreational mariners. But to owners of small boats, a lighthouse is still a valuable visual aid, a welcome sight in a storm, and a guide past treacherous rocks, reefs, and shoals, just as it was when hardy keepers maintained the lights.

There is good reason for the old lighthouse saying: there is no such thing as a fat keeper. These men—and women who often inherited the job when their husbands drowned, died, ran away, or went mad—had to haul oil up the tower's twisting stairs in huge cans. Twice a night, sometimes in raging storms, deep fog, and cold mists, they trudged up to reset the optical mechanism. There were wicks to be trimmed and lit—hence lighthouse keepers' "wickies" nickname—reflectors to be polished, soot to be cleaned from lenses, and the fog signal to be maintained. Because of the importance of lighthouses as daymarks, they also had to be kept freshly painted in a variety of distinctive patterns. And when mariners foundered nearby, the lightkeeper felt duty-bound to rescue them. Dozens of keepers drowned trying.

Wood fires illuminated early lighthouses. Arrays of candles arranged in tiers, and coal in brazier pans, were also tried. Then came whale- and fish-oil lamps, which produced a terrible stench. Even worse was colza oil from rapeseed. "Smelled like cooking cabbage," noted Scott Stanton, a boatswain's mate and one of the keepers at the Coast Guard's last staffed station at Boston Light. This was also the nation's first lighthouse, erected by the Massachusetts Bay Colony in 1716.

French physicist Augustin-Jean Fresnel revolutionized the lighthouse in 1822 with a system that took advantage of the refractive properties of glass. The Fresnel lens bent a single light source inside a beehive of glass prisms into powerful sheets visible up to twenty-two miles away. The old Lighthouse Service designed a different signaling pattern for each and every light. In 1939 President Franklin Roosevelt, concerned about wartime readiness, placed light stations under the Coast Guard. The move spelled the end of the Lighthouse Service and to the staffing of most towers.

Even the sturdiest of lighthouses could not survive all of the ravages of nature and man. Some have succumbed to relentless erosion. Ice floes took out others. Before park services and historical societies came to the rescue, the Coast Guard rapidly decommissioned lighthouses, leaving them to whatever fate might befall them. It was open season for pranksters, pyromaniacs, and vandals.

During the heyday of the U.S. Lighthouse Service, when 1,462 light stations ringed America's shorelines, Fresnel lenses were brought to a depot on Staten Island, New York, where they were assembled for shipment to light stations around the country. Abandoned in the 1960s, the facility sat idle until 1999, when the site, with a spectacular Manhattan view, was selected for a new national lighthouse museum.

But each lighthouse is its own treasured historic curiosity. These towers' austere beauty, keepers' lonely stories, and fanciful tales of lighthouse hauntings have inspired books and poems, paintings, collectable ceramic miniatures, license plates, and postage stamps. Many structures remain endangered, but the nation's affection for these beacons in the night shines brightly.

OVERLEAF: In 1827, President John Quincy Adams commissioned a lighthouse on a Pemaquid Point promontory high above Muscongus Bay on the central Maine coast. Inside the keeper's house, the town of Bristol operates a fisherman's museum that catalogues stories of Maine lighthouses and shipwrecks offshore. Pemaquid's light was the state's first to be automated in 1934.

Fog nearly obscures the Rockland Breakwater Light (above) off Maine's
Jameson Point. The nearly mile-long jetty is made of carved lime rock slabs,
carefully arranged jigsaw-puzzle fashion. These rocks were a principal
export from Rockland in the late nineteenth century. Owls Head Light
(opposite) overlooks the opposite end of the harbor. A legendary springer
spaniel that once rang the station's fog bell when he spotted an approach-
ing vessel is buried—with proper commemoration—on the property.

Portland Head Light (opposite), in Maine's largest city, once inspired the Henry Wadsworth Longfellow poem, "The Lighthouse." This is a contender for the honor as America's most-painted lighthouse. Portland's breakwater light (left) is a "bug"-style light. Once decrepit, the lighthouse was restored as a community-service project by the Rotary Club of South Portland. The westernmost of the "Two Lights" (above) in Cape Elizabeth, Maine, is now a private residence, off-limits to visitors.

Maine's 1877 cast-iron Cape Neddick Light (opposite) is better known as the "Nubble" lighthouse. A nubble is a small knob—in this case a little lump of an island. A magnificent lighthouse (left) rises atop the famous—but fragile and eroding—cliffs of Gay Head on Martha's Vineyard in Massachusetts. There is a small admission charge every day it is open to visitors, save one: on Mother's Day.

The 1865 Fresnel lens and clockworks
(above), taken from the Gay Head Light,
is a featured attraction of the Martha's Vineyard
Historical Society in Edgartown. Cape Poge
Lighthouse (left) stands amid a wildlife refuge
on Chappaquiddick Island off Martha's
Vineyard. The lighthouse, maintained by
a private, nonprofit organization called the
Trustees of Reservations, can be reached
across shifting dunes only after one reduces
an automobile's tire pressure by two-thirds.

The old keeper's desk (above) is one
of many artifacts that have been preserved
in the Rose Island Lighthouse in Rhode Island's
Narragansett Bay, overlooking Newport.
Arrangements can be made for an overnight
stay as part of an ecological experience that
includes careful monitoring of energy and water
use, food composting, and beach clean-up. The
lighthouse (right) sent out a steady red beam
from 1869 until 1971, when a series of lights was
incorporated into a new bridge across the bay.

The 1796 Montauk Point Light (left), commissioned by George Washington, was many immigrants' first sight of America as their ships approached New York Harbor. Minus its lamp, the 1824 stone tower of the harbor lighthouse (above) in Stonington, Connecticut, is now operated as a lighthouse museum by Stonington Village's Historical Society. The old light (overleaf) atop Battery Weed at Fort Wadsworth on Staten Island was completed during the Civil War.

This staircase (opposite) has been refurbished as part of an extensive renovation of the 1857 Absecon Light in Atlantic City. Before casinos, the lighthouse bathed the famous beach resort in light.

It takes 217 steps to scale "Old Barney"—New Jersey's 170-foot-tall Barnegat Lighthouse (top left). A four-story square tower pokes through the keeper's dwelling at the Victorian Hereford Inlet Light (bottom left) in North Wildwood, New Jersey.

Cheesebox-shaped Seven Foot Knoll Lighthouse (above), now on display
in the glittering Inner Harbor of Baltimore, Maryland, shone when the
harbor was a grimy industrial area. This is a squat "screwpile"-style light.
Also in Baltimore Harbor is the Lightship Chesapeake (opposite), originally
launched in 1930. The ship, which guided vessels into Chesapeake
Bay, has also served as a harbor patrol boat and a floating educational
classroom. It's now part of the Baltimore Maritime Museum.

Built of local brick in 1828, Cove Point Light (opposite) at the entrance to the Patuxent River is Maryland's oldest operating lighthouse. Keepers at Drum Point Light, now an exhibit of the Calvert Marine Museum in Solomons, Maryland, had many of the comforts of a cozy cottage (left). Hexagaonal Drum Point (overleaf) is another screwpile light. Its wrought-iron pilings were screwed into the bedrock of the Chesapeake Bay.

In 1999, the strikingly striped Cape Hatteras Light (opposite), perhaps the nation's best-known light tower, was gingerly moved more than twenty-nine hundred feet farther from the encroaching sea on that North Carolina barrier island. Picturesque Ocracoke Island's lighthouse (left) can be reached only by private boat or one of North Carolina's many ferries. This light has functioned continuously since 1864, when a lens destroyed by Confederate forces was replaced.

One of America's newest lighthouses is Harbour Town Light (above),
built on Hilton Head Island, South Carolina, in 1970. The Lighthouse has
become a symbol of the island's Sea Pines Resort. Haig Point Light
(opposite) on South Carolina's Daufuskie Island, was restored by the
International Paper Realty Corporation as a bed-and-breakfast inn for
members and guests of the Haig Point Club. Its privately maintained light
marks the confluence of the Intracoastal Waterway and Calibogue Sound.

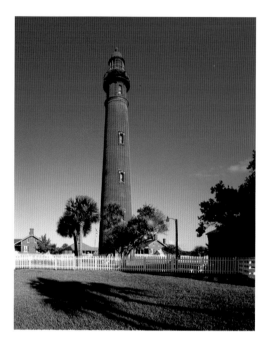

One of America's oldest brick lighthouses is Ponce de Leon Inlet Lighthouse (above), south of Daytona Beach, Florida. At 175 feet, it is also one of the tallest. Hillsboro Inlet Light (right), marking the northern approach to Miami, is anchored by giant pilings. Built in Chicago, the lighthouse was exhibited at the 1904 World's Fair in Saint Louis before being dismantled and shipped to Florida. The Cape Florida Lighthouse (overleaf) overlooking Biscayne Bay was extensively renovated following Hurricane Andrew in 1992.

The 1831 Saint Marks Light (opposite) towers over the wetlands of a national wildlife refuge on Florida's Panhandle. The little New Canal Light (top left) stands on a Lake Pontchartrain pier in New Orleans, Louisiana. The lighthouse was intended to mark a canal to downtown that was never built. A faux lighthouse (bottom left) in New Orleans once, appropriately, housed an office of the Lighthouse for the Blind.

1 Duluth North Breakwater Minn 1910

2 Split Rock Minn 1910

3 Rock of Ages Minn 1908

4 Eagle Harbor Mich 1871

5 White Shoals Mich 1910

6 Spectacle Reef Mich 1874

7 Sturgeon Bay Canal Wi 1903

8 Wind Point Wisc 1880

9 Chicago Harbor Ill 1843

10 Michigan City In 1858

11 Big Sable Mich 1867

12 Harbor Beach Mich 1885

13 Marblehead Ohio 1821

14 Lorain Ohio 1909

15 Presque Isle Pa. 1872

16 Old Buffalo Harbor NY 1836

17 Charlotte-Genesee NY 1822

18 Galloo Island NY 1867

Map Legend
1 Duluth North
   Breakwater Mn   1910
2 Split Rock Mn   1910
3 Rock of Ages Mn   1908
4 Eagle Harbor Mi   1871
5 White Shoal Mi   1910
6 Spectacle Reef Mi 1874
7 Sturgeon Bay
   Canal Wi   1903
8 Wind Point Wi   1880
9 Chicago Harbor Il 1843
10 Michigan City In 1858
11 Big Sable Mi   1867
12 Harbor Beach Mi   1885
13 Marble Head Oh   1821
14 Lorain Oh   1909
15 Presque Isle Pa   1872
16 Buffalo NY   1836
17 Charlotte-
   Genesee NY   1822
18 Galloo Island NY 1867

A quilted wall hanging (opposite) by Mary Lou Miller depicts several Great Lakes lighthouses. It hangs in the Charlotte-Genesee Lighthouse in Rochester, New York. That 1822 structure (left) was erected on an old Indian Campground at the spot where residents of "Charlotte" fought off British invaders during the War of 1812. An old cast-iron staircase (above) can be climbed at the Thirty Mile Point Lighthouse in Golden Hill State Park, overlooking Lake Ontario near Barker, New York.

From 1875 to 1885, Thirty Mile Point Lighthouse overlooking Lake Ontario in New York was illuminated by a kerosene lantern, which keeper Robert Bannerman routinely cleaned with this horsehair brush (above). The kerosene was stored in a separate structure still standing apart from the tower. The lighthouse (left) is now administered by the New York State Parks system, which extensively renovated the historic building in the mid-1990s.

The South Pierhead Lighthouse (above)—
"Big Red"—in Holland Harbor, Michigan,
was rescued by citizens in 1970 when the Coast
Guard wanted to abandon it. Appropriately,
in this city famous for its tulip festival, the lighthouse's gabled roof reflects the city's Dutch
influence. The 1904 East Pierhead Lighthouse
(right) in Michigan City is Indiana's only
publicly accessible operating lighthouse.
The 1870 Point Iroquois Light Station
(overleaf) in Upper Michigan's Hiawatha
National Forest stands at the point on Lake
Superior where Chippewa Indians halted
the rival Iroquois' westward expansion.

Big Bay Point Lighthouse (above), north of Marquette, Michigan, is a working lighthouse and an active bed-and-breakfast inn. Guests stay in the keepers' and assistants' old rooms, many with views of Lake Superior. The 1892 Seul Choix Point Lighthouse (right), near Gulliver on the upper Lake Michigan peninsula, helps guide boaters through the dangerous Straits of Macinaw. The name, translated as "Only Choice" in English, refers to a landing in a fierce storm by French sailors in the years when Upper Michigan was French territory.

The Two Harbors Agate Bay Lighthouse (above) in Minnesota was
built in 1892. The Lake County Historical Society operates a museum there
with displays about fishing, lighthouses, and shipwrecks in the region.
Up the road is the majestic Split Rock Lighthouse (overleaf), whose
fog-signal building (opposite) is filled with artifacts and exhibits. Lifting
310 tons of building materials to the lighthouse construction site atop
a rugged 130-foot cliff in 1909–10 took incredible engineering acumen.

At Fort Rodd Hill Canadian National Historic Park near Victoria, British Columbia, stands Fisgard Lighthouse (opposite), the first permanent lighthouse on Vancouver Island's western shore. Illuminated by the British in 1860, it was automated in 1928. Uphill are gun emplacements that guarded Victoria and the Esquimalt Naval Base. The Sequim-Dungeness Valley Chamber of Commerce on Washington's Olympic Peninsula displays a model of the nearby New Dungeness Lighthouse (above).

Battery Point Lighthouse (left) once guided lumber ships into and out of the harbor in Crescent City, California, on the Oregon border. The lighthouse miraculously survived not only vicious poundings from Pacific storms but also five successive tidal waves that inundated the town following a cataclysmic Alaska earthquake. Haceta Head Lighthouse (above) in Oregon, managed by the U.S. Forest Service, was named for Spanish explorer Don Bruno de Haceta.

Trinidad Head Lighthouse in Northern
California is closed to the public. But in 1949
the Trinidad Civic Club built this near-identical
replica (above), equipped with a Fresnel lens
that once shone from the original structure.
A tiny light tower (right) was part of the
fortifications at Fort Point beneath the southern
anchorage of San Francisco's Golden Gate
Bridge. The U.S. Corps of Engineers constructed
the fort in 1855 from more than eight million
bricks as well as granite shipped from China.

Old Point Loma Lighthouse (opposite), high above San Diego Harbor, was abandoned in 1891 in favor of a lower, more convenient replacement. Restoration began in 1933 as part of the creation of Cabrillo National Monument to honor the Spanish explorer who discovered present-day California. A park superintendent now lives in the gingerbread Point Fermin Lighthouse (above) fronting Los Angeles Harbor. Point Montara Lighthouse (overleaf), south of San Francisco, is now a European-style hostel.

Coast Guard Boatswain's Mate 1st Class
Scott Stanton polishes the Second Order Fresnel
lens at Boston Light, America's first lighthouse.
The lighthouse, on Little Brewster Island, has
guided ships to safe harbor since 1716. Blown up
by the British in 1776, it was rebuilt in 1783
by Governor John Hancock. By congressional
decree, Boston Light shall remain "forever
manned" by active-duty Coast Guard personnel
as a tribute to the nation's distinguished Coast
Guard and U.S. Lighthouse Service tradition.